SO MUCH MORE TO HELEN!

The Passions and Pursuits of Helen Keller

Written by
MEEG PINCUS

Illustrated by
CAROLINE BONNE-MÜLLER

PUBLISHED BY SLEEPING BEAR PRESS

Asked of Helen Keller's glory,
most folks talk of this one story:
DeafBlind girl—no one could reach her.
First word "water," thanks to teacher.
It's (mostly) true and worth retellin'—
yet there's so much more to Helen!

Helen Keller is the most famous DeafBlind American in history. She's best known for the moment she first understood sign language, when her teacher finger-spelled "water" into her hand at the family water pump. (True, though she'd already created about 60 of her own gestures to communicate.) Beyond that celebrated scene, Helen was also many more things. . . .

Helen was a friend . . .

To her playmate and her mentor.
Then First Lady and inventor.

Helen's first friend was a girl named Martha, who played, baked, and quarreled
with Helen in the Kellers' yard and kitchen. As Helen grew up, she was closest
with her teacher and mentor, Annie Sullivan, and had well-known friends including
First Lady Eleanor Roosevelt and inventor Alexander Graham Bell.

Helen was an adventurer...

Splashing, riding, asking questions.
New encounters, bold suggestions.

She darted into the ocean her first time at the beach.
After tumbling in the waves, she emerged demanding,
"Who put salt in the water?!" Helen wasn't afraid to
express her opinions or try new things (like hot dogs
and horseback riding, which she loved!).

Helen was a student...

Reading, writing, craving knowledge.

She was constantly reading and could understand English, French, and German. Once, she entered a book editor's office and, just from the smell, signed, "Oh, the books, the books, so many, many books. How lovely!" She became the first DeafBlind person to graduate from college in the United States.

Braille and signing, first through college.

Helen was a dog lover...

Cherished canines of all sizes.
True companions, great surprises.

She always had beloved dogs by her side, from Scotties to Great Danes. She wrote that if she was granted sight, the first thing she'd do is look into her dog's eyes. She brought the first Akita to the United States, a gift from the government of Japan.

Helen was an author...

Always writing, never slowing.
Essays, books, and stories flowing.

She loved to write and listed "author" as her profession on her passport. She published 14 books and 475 other writings, starting with fictional stories in childhood, then writing about her thoughts and experiences throughout her life. Her first book, *The Story of My Life,* is still read worldwide.

Helen was an activist...

Workers' rights and women voting.
Anti-racist, peace promoting.

She was passionate about peace, justice, and equality for all. She marched for women's right to vote and for better working conditions, especially for children. She spoke out against racism, poverty, and war—standing by her values even when many people disagreed with her.

Helen was a jokester...

Clever comments, joyful laughter.
Witty wordplay, smiling after.

She had a quick, mischievous sense of humor. Her dear friend, the famous humor writer Mark Twain, wrote that Helen could keep up with any joking at a party, saying: "She is almost certain to send back as good as she gets, and almost as certainly with an improvement added."

Helen was a performer...

Big-screen movies, old-time stages.
Five years touring, earning wages.

When she and Annie Sullivan needed money in the 1920s, they created a stage act of their story (with an orchestra!) to pay their bills. Helen also starred in two Hollywood silent films about her life, winning an Oscar for one.

Helen was a romantic...

One true love, their hearts committed.
Dreams of marriage not permitted.

She fell in love with a journalist named Peter Fagan, who shared her activist values and asked her to marry him. But Helen's family believed, as many people did then, that DeafBlind people should not marry or have children. So they sent Peter away.

Helen was a survivor...

Discrimination, heartbreak, grieving.
Never gave up, kept believing.

She mourned over Peter, then the deaths of her teacher Annie and her parents, then her house burning down. She faced insults about her disabilities from some who disagreed with her. She felt discouraged, angry, and lonely at times, but always carried on—and lived to age 88.

Helen was a traveler...

Forty countries, filling theaters.
Soothing soldiers, meeting leaders.

She traveled to five of the seven continents as a humanitarian and peacemaker. After the World Wars, she visited wounded soldiers and damaged cities to help foster goodwill and healing. She gave speeches in packed amphitheaters and met with world leaders as well as everyday struggling people.

Helen was a changemaker...

Fought for those with deafness, blindness.
Laws, employment, schools—and kindness.

Much of her life's work was advocating for people with disabilities, especially the DeafBlind. She lobbied U.S. states, presidents, and Congress to support schools and job training for people with disabilities, for she felt the opportunity to work was most important for their well-being. She inspired compassion and understanding.

Helen was—
as we all are—

so many things!

Helen Keller sent the world a message that endures today: People with disabilities—visible and invisible ones—have so much to offer! All of these accomplished, passionate people also have/had disabilities—turn the page to find their names.

MORE TO HELEN'S STORY
Further Explanation of Each Spread

DEAFBLIND: Helen Keller lost her hearing and sight from an illness as a toddler. Most people think she then could not communicate at all until age six when her teacher, Annie Sullivan, broke through to her by finger-spelling W-A-T-E-R into her hand at the water pump. This story of Helen is the one most people remember about her. (There's even a statue of Helen at the water pump in the U.S. Capitol!) However, while Helen passionately credited her teacher with opening the wide world of words and language to her, she did communicate before that famous moment, with about 60 gestures she created to make herself understood by her family and her playmate Martha Washington.

FRIEND: Helen had friends of all ages throughout her life, including her first friend, Martha, whose mother worked as a chef for the Kellers, with whom she fed chickens, rolled dough, and often quarreled! She had lifelong friendships with her beloved teacher Annie Sullivan, the writer Mark Twain (who helped get her a scholarship to college), telephone inventor Alexander Graham Bell (who had deaf family members and taught in the deaf community), First Lady Eleanor Roosevelt (with whom Helen shared political passions), and others. She built relationships with them through writing letters and feeling their hands, facial expressions, throat vibrations, and lip movements when visiting with them in person.

ADVENTURER: Helen famously wrote: "Life is either a daring adventure or nothing." She wanted to experience all of life that she could, from her travels to making movies to flying in an open-cockpit airplane. She also wanted the world to know that people with disabilities could experience so much more than many at her time believed, including athletic activities, passionate relationships, and meaningful work.

STUDENT: Helen was a star student from age eight at the Perkins School for the Blind in Massachusetts. After four years of immensely hard work by her and Annie to translate books and lectures into fingerspelling, she became the first person with DeafBlindness to graduate from college in the United States in 1904. And not just any college, but Radcliffe, the sister school to prestigious Harvard; and not just graduated, but graduated with honors (excellent grades)!

DOG LOVER: Helen had many dog companions of various breeds throughout her life, and they brought her much joy. She's credited with bringing the Akita Japanese breed of dog to the United States, after the Japanese government gifted her one on her 1937 visit to Japan. (By the way, she also had other pets at times, including a donkey, a rooster, a cat, and a protective pet monkey!)

AUTHOR: Helen longed to be an author from a young age, always writing stories and letters. Writing was her passion and she loved to type on her typewriter about her inner thoughts and outer adventures. She published 14 books and more than 475 essays and speeches in her life. Her autobiography, *The Story of My Life,* has been translated into 50 languages and is still in print today.

ACTIVIST: Helen wrote often about her political beliefs and was an activist for women's suffrage (voting rights), civil rights (equality for people of color), workers' rights (including stopping child labor), healthcare (especially for women and children), anti-war causes, and more. She was a very early supporter of two major civil rights groups—the NAACP, an anti-racist group, and the ACLU, a freedom of speech group she co-founded. American society was segregated by race in Helen's time, especially in the South where she was raised, but she grew up to speak out against racism. She was also a member of the Socialist Party—a political group that opposed the economic system of the United States, because they believed it created poor working and living conditions for many, while a few got very rich.

JOKESTER: Helen was known among her friends for her quick (sometimes wicked) sense of humor and wit. She loved to have fun with words. She also used humor in her writings, her stage act, and speeches. To deal with uncomfortable situations, she often used jokes with people who challenged her.

PERFORMER: Helen starred in two Hollywood silent films about her life. She even won an Oscar for one of them, *Helen Keller in Her Story*, in 1955 (though she missed the film's opening to protest with actors demanding better working conditions)! She is the only person in history to win an Oscar for a film about herself, then have someone playing her win an Oscar many years later (Patty Duke in *The Miracle Worker*). Helen mostly enjoyed her five years touring as a vaudeville (old-time stage theater) act. Helen would sign, Annie (then later, Polly Thomson) would speak aloud, and then they would take audience questions.

ROMANTIC: Helen longed for love and romantic companionship her whole life. When she was 36 years old, a newspaper journalist named Peter Fagan was hired to help care for Helen while Annie was ill. Peter also shared Helen's passionate political beliefs. The two fell in love and wanted to marry. Sadly, during that time most people with disabilities were discouraged from marrying and having children. Helen's "love-dream was shattered" when her family forbade her marriage and pushed Peter out of her life.

SURVIVOR: Along with the loss of Peter, Helen had several other heartbreaks in her life. She was devastated at age 11 when she was accused of copying her first published story from an existing children's book, and she almost stopped writing after that. Later in her life, when Helen wrote about her political beliefs, many of the same journalists who'd once praised her brilliance then called her mentally challenged. She also faced the deaths of her closest loved ones: her parents and her teacher Annie, and the loss of her home to a fire (including all of her diaries and letters from Annie and Peter). After each hurt, Helen carried on—she wrote again, she kept speaking up for her beliefs, and she lived a long life!

TRAVELER: Helen traveled throughout the United States and 39 other countries. She was given humanitarian awards from Brazil, Japan, and the Philippines. She traveled abroad well into her elder years. One of the most meaningful tours she took was visiting wounded soldiers, especially those who were blinded, at 70 Army hospitals around the United States during World War II. She also visited blinded soldiers during World War I and the Korean War, and visited the Japanese cities destroyed in World War II by American nuclear bombs (which she spoke out against).

CHANGEMAKER: Helen made many strides toward laws, programs, and inclusion of people with DeafBlindness and other disabilities. (Though she also has a complicated legacy within disabilities activism, as she was always set apart as a single example and she supported some theories now disregarded.) She met or corresponded with nine U.S. presidents in her lifetime, from Grover Cleveland to Lyndon B. Johnson; was nominated for the Nobel Peace Prize; and received the highest American honor, the Presidential Medal of Freedom.

SO MANY THINGS: Today, people with both visible and invisible disabilities know that every part of us makes us who we are. Helen Keller exemplified this and should be known as the accomplished, multifaceted person she was. Just like these amazing folks:

1. Frida Kahlo (painter with chronic pain, childhood polio, and injury) **2. Sonia Sotomayor** (Supreme Court Justice with diabetes) **3. Stevie Wonder** (musician/songwriter who is blind) **4. Simone Biles** (pro gymnast with ADHD) **5. Selena Gomez** (singer/actor with lupus, mental health conditions) **6. Danny Glover** (film actor with dyslexia, childhood epilepsy) **7. Wanda Díaz-Merced** (astronomer who is blind) **8. Pablo Pineda** (actor/writer with Down syndrome) **9. Greta Thunberg** (climate change activist with autism) **10. Haben Girma** (disability rights lawyer who is DeafBlind) **11. Naomi Osaka** (pro tennis player with anxiety, depression) **12. Jerome Bettis** (pro football player with asthma, anaphylactic food allergy) **13. Ali Stroker** (stage actor who uses a wheelchair)

AUTHOR'S NOTE

For my high school senior passion project, I read stacks of Helen Keller's writings and wrote a stage play about her. I had learned to use American Sign Language with Deaf friends at my integrated hearing/Deaf middle school and loved learning about Deaf culture. Mostly, though, I chose Helen because she inspired me as I tried to integrate my own invisible disabilities (including fibromyalgia, a chronic pain/gastrointestinal condition) into my life and identity.

Reading Helen's little-known works opened me up to so much more about her than I'd been taught. Most especially, her passions for social justice, politics, and activism were just the messages I needed as I chose my own life path.

I wanted to offer today's kids the fuller picture of Helen that I got by digging more deeply into her life. I believe she'd want you to know about her adventurousness, humor, heartbreaks, and, probably above all, her politics. I also believe she'd want you to know that today people with disabilities (particularly people of color) face twice as much poverty and joblessness as people without disabilities—there's much work to be done.

Helen Keller was a full, complicated human being, like all of us. She was also what I call a "solutionary": someone trying to solve problems for people, animals, and the planet. I hope this book inspires you—whatever disabilities or challenges you may face—to follow your own passions and be a solutionary, too.

To Merle Preston—with gratitude for 39 years of sisterly support on my health and life journeys.
And to Sarah Rockett—with gratitude for 6 years of editor-ly support on my kidlit writing journey.
—M.P.

To tante Han, who is always there for me
—C.B.M.

Text Copyright © 2022 Meeg Pincus
Illustration Copyright © 2022 Caroline Bonne-Müller
Design Copyright © 2022 Sleeping Bear Press

SLEEPING BEAR PRESS™

2395 South Huron Parkway, Suite 200
Ann Arbor, MI 48104
www.sleepingbearpress.com

Printed and bound in the United States.

10 9 8 7 6 5 4 3 2 1

Library of Congress Cataloging-in-Publication Data on file

Photo credits: Library of Congress, C. M. Bell Collection, LOC Control No: 2016691950, back cover; Library of Congress, LOC Control No: 2002706669, page 30

Quotation References: *"Who put salt in the water?!"* —Keller, Helen. *The Story of My Life.* Signet Classic Edition: 1988. Pg. 36. | *"Oh, the books, the books, so many books! How lovely!"* —Twain, Mark. *Autobiography of Mark Twain, Volume 1: The Complete and Authoritative Edition.* University of California Press, 2010. Pg. 465. | *"She is almost certain to send back as good as she gets . . ."* —Twain, Mark. *Autobiography of Mark Twain, Volume 2: The Complete and Authoritative Edition.* University of California Press, 2013. Pg. 375. | *"Life is either a daring adventure or nothing."* —Keller, Helen. *The Open Door.* Doubleday: 1957. Pg. 27. | *"love-dream shattered"* —Keller, Helen. *Midstream: My Later Life.* Doubleday: 1929. Pg. 223.
Additional Selected Sources: Keller, Helen. *Out of the Dark: Essays, Lectures, and Addresses on Physical and Social Vision.* Forgotten Books: July 29, 2012. | Perkins School for the Blind and American Foundation for the Blind online Helen Keller archives. | Lawlor, Laurie. *Helen Keller: Rebellious Spirit.* Holiday House: 2001. | Echner, Kat. "Three Big Ableist Myths About the Life of Helen Keller." *Smithsonian Magazine.* June 27, 2017. | For full bibliography, see Teaching Guide: sleepingbearpress.com/teaching_guides.